Meet the
Samuel Far[...]

— 3 —

Martha is Afraid of the Dark

Jesus said:
"I am the light of the world."

A party was going on
at Auntie Dinah's house.
Everyone was there to see the
new baby.
"We're going to call him Benjamin,"
said Uncle Jonas.
Dan, Martha and Matthew thought
that was a good name.

It was a good party too.
There were dates and figs and
honey cakes to eat, and all kinds
of nuts to nibble.
Everyone was talking and laughing.

It was late when the party ended.
Matthew had fallen asleep,
curled up on the floor.
Mr Samuel had to carry him home
and put him to bed.

"I'm so full, I couldn't eat one more nut," said Martha.
"Greedy!" teased Dan. "You'll have bad dreams."
"Go to sleep now, both of you," said Dad.

In the middle of the night
Martha suddenly woke up.
She *had* had a bad dream.
And something was wrong.
The room was quite dark.
The lamp had gone out!
Usually it burned all night.
But Mrs Samuel had been so tired
after the party that she had
forgotten to fill it with oil.

Martha began to feel frightened.
She could hear something moving.
She held her breath and listened.
Next moment she felt something tugging at the end of her sleeping-mat.
She gave a little scream.

"Mummy! Mummy! There's a monster pulling at my mat."
Mrs Samuel woke up at once.
"It's just a bad dream," she said.
But then *she* heard a funny noise.

Mr Samuel was awake by now.
"Why, the lamp has gone out,"
he said. "We must have forgotten
to fill it."
He felt his way to the lampstand
and then to the jar of oil.
"I'll have to go next door
to light the lamp," he said.
"Let's hope the Levis remembered
to fill theirs."
All the time he was gone
the strange noises continued.
Martha couldn't think what was
making them.

Then Dad was back.
Warm lamplight filled the room,
chasing away the blackness.
Mr Samuel began to laugh.
"There's your monster," he said,
pointing to the end of Martha's
sleeping-mat.
Martha and Mrs Samuel stared.
Then they began to laugh, too.
For there was Matthew's pet goat,
quietly nibbling Martha's mat.

Now that the light was shining
Martha wasn't a bit afraid.
She led the goat back to its place
and tied it up.

"Settle down, now," said Mum,
"and go back to sleep."
Martha wrapped herself up warmly
and snuggled down. She felt
happy and peaceful and sleepy again.
She looked across at the little
lamp. How scarey it had been
in the dark. The light had made
everything all right again.
They must never, never let it
go out.

Martha was afraid of the dark.
How glad she was when the lamp
made the room light again.

Jesus said:
"I am the light of the world."
Jesus is like the lamp. With him
we can see our way,
so we need never be frightened.